Amphibians

Salamanders

by Molly Kolpin

Consulting editor: Gail Saunders-Smith, PhD

Consultant: Linda Weir
USGS Patuxent Wildlife Research Center
Laurel, Maryland

CAPSTONE PRESS
a capstone imprint

Pebble Plus is published by Capstone Press,
151 Good Counsel Drive, P.O. Box 669, Mankato, Minnesota 56002.
www.capstonepress.com

092009
005618CGS10

 Books published by Capstone Press are manufactured with paper
containing at least 10 percent post-consumer waste.

Library of Congress Cataloging-in-Publication Data
Kolpin, Molly.
    Salamanders / by Molly Kolpin.
        p. cm. — (Pebble plus. Amphibians)
    Includes bibliographical references and index.
    Summary: "Simple text and photographs present salamanders, how they look, where they live,
and what they do" — Provided by publisher.
        ISBN 978-1-4296-3990-3 (library binding)
        ISBN 978-1-4296-4851-6 (paperback)
1. Salamanders — Juvenile literature. I. Title.
QL668.C2K655 2010
597.8'5 — dc22   2009027065

Editorial Credits
Jenny Marks, editor; Lori Bye, designer; Marcie Spence, media researcher; Eric Manske, production specialist

All diagram illustrations in this book are by Kristin Kest.

Photo Credits
Dreamstime/Chrisjo88, 1; Mike_kiev, cover; Pro777, 9
iStockphoto/Fibena, 7; tcd004, 5
Peter Arnold/Biosphotos/Delobelle Jean-Philippe, 21; Matt Meadows, 13, 17; WILDLIFE, 15
Shutterstock/Anita Huszti, 11

Note to Parents and Teachers

The Amphibians set supports national science standards related to life science. This book
describes and illustrates salamanders. The images support early readers in understanding
the text. The repetition of words and phrases helps early readers learn new words. This book
also introduces early readers to subject-specific vocabulary words, which are defined in the
Glossary section. Early readers may need assistance to read some words and to use the Table of
Contents, Glossary, Read More, Internet Sites, and Index sections of the book.

Table of Contents

All Kinds of Salamanders

Salamanders are

wet-skinned amphibians.

A salamander's skin

can be smooth or bumpy.

Some have spots or stripes.

There are more than
500 kinds of salamanders.
Most are 2 to 8 inches
(5 to 20 centimeters) long.

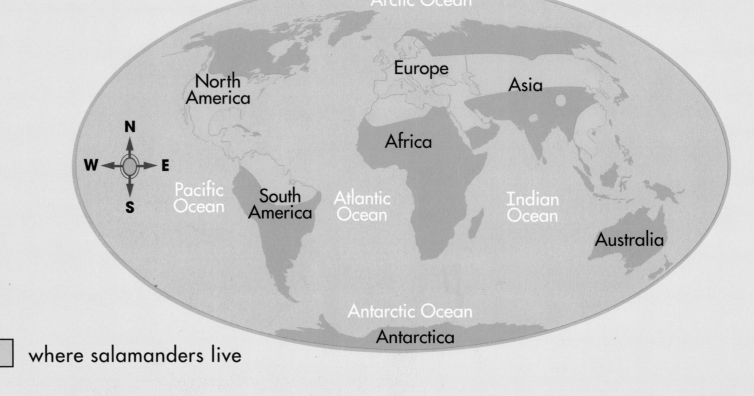

where salamanders live

Salamanders live on land
or in water.
Some live in both places.
All salamanders must keep
their skin cool and wet.

Land and Water

On land, salamanders

walk on four short legs.

Each foot has tiny toes.

Some salamanders spend
their whole lives underwater.
They breathe in the water
using gills.

gill

What's for Dinner?

Salamanders hunt at night.

Most land salamanders

sneak up on their prey.

They catch worms and bugs

with their long, sticky tongues.

A Salamander's Life

Most salamanders lay eggs.

Some lay their eggs

in moist areas on land.

Others lay eggs in water.

eggs

Young salamanders
are called larvae.

They look a little like tadpoles.

The larvae grow legs
as they become adults.

Mole Salamander Life Cycle

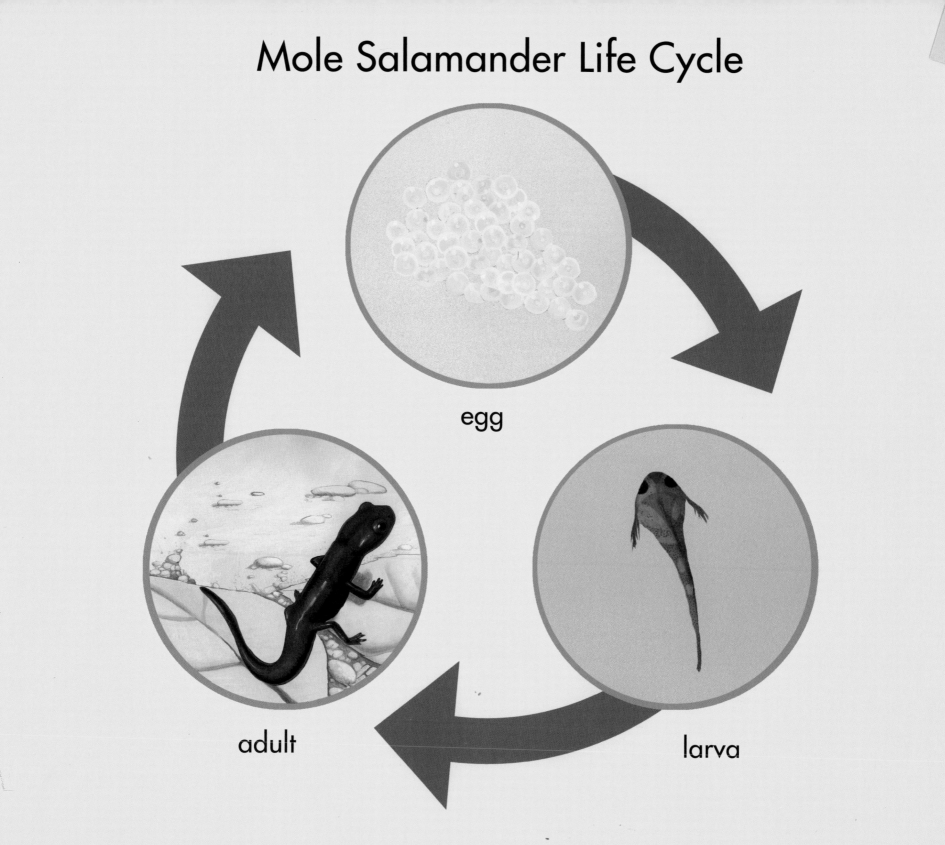

egg

larva

adult

Wild salamanders live
up to 30 years.
In places like zoos,
salamanders can live
for more than 50 years.

Glossary

amphibian — a cold-blooded animal with a backbone and wet skin

burrow — a hole in the ground used by an animal

gill — a part of the body used to take oxygen from water; salamanders that live in the water breathe through gills.

larva — a young salamander that lives underwater

moist — slightly wet

prey — an animal hunted by other animals for food

Read More

Nelson, Robin. *Salamanders.* Animal Life Cycles. Minneapolis: Lerner, 2009.

Winnick, Nick. *Salamanders.* Backyard Animals. New York: Weigl, 2010.

Internet Sites

FactHound offers a safe, fun way to find Internet sites related to this book. All of the sites on FactHound have been researched by our staff.

Here's all you do:

Visit *www.facthound.com*

FactHound will fetch the best sites for you!

Index

Word Count: 167
Grade: 1
Early-Intervention Level: 17